Anthony J.D. Biddle

Shantytown Sketches

Anthony J.D. Biddle

Shantytown Sketches

ISBN/EAN: 9783337092726

Printed in Europe, USA, Canada, Australia, Japan

Cover: Foto ©ninafisch / pixelio.de

More available books at **www.hansebooks.com**

IN THE FASHIONABLE QUARTER.

Shantytown Sketches

BY

ANTHONY J. DREXEL BIDDLE

Author of "A Dual Role and Other Stories," etc.

ILLUSTRATED BY

CLARENCE SNYDER

[*Sixth Edition*]

PHILADELPHIA :

DREXEL BIDDLE, PUBLISHER
WALNUT STREET

1899

To my Brother
Livingston Ludlow Biddle

CONTENTS

DOWN SHAMROCK ALLEY

MIT VRIENDS

MEETINGS OF THE GRAND WATERMELON-PATCH DEBATING SOCIETY

ILLUSTRATIONS

DOWN SHAMROCK ALLEY

Mrs. Mulhooney's Receiving Day

.

MRS. MULHOONEY'S RECEPTION.

"GOOD afthernoon, Mrs. Mulhooney, an' this is yer day fer resavin', is it?"

"Ah moy, an' is thot you, Mrs. O'Conner? Yis this is moy day 'to home,' an' it's glad Oi be to see you. Take a seat by the foire here, an' come in! An' how be yez shtanding the atmosphere this cloimate?"

"Oh! It's doyin' Oi am, Mrs. Mulhooney!"

"Aye, yer face looks ill, Mrs. O'Conner. Ye should take a roide in thim new electhric cars wot runs on Catharine Street now. Begob, it's a great thing fer Philadelphie to hov thim—an' on'y five cents too, Mrs. O'Conner, fer a nice afthernoon's roide from wan ind av the metrolopus to the other. It would do yer health good to take one, fer indade it was on'y yisterday thot Pat says ter me: 'Faith, an' Mrs. O'Conner looks es if she were goin' ter be the cause of a "wake" soon,' an' he was roight, fer indade yer look kinder thot way."

"Faith, Mrs. Mulhooney, an' it's a roight comfortin' an' sympathitic friend yez are—an' how is Pat doin' now?"

13

"Oh, foinly, Mrs. O'Conner; he's struck a job av wurrk over to Wist Philadelphic wid an' 'upper ten family.' "

"An' phwat's he doin' there?"

"Roiding on the top av a carriage all over the city, as if he owned the whole concern, wid the Misses sittin' quoiet loike insoide, an' he's gettin' thot shtuck up, Mrs. O'Conner, ez he wouldn't aven take aff his hat whin he drove past me the other day, an' me his woife, too. He tould me aftherwards thot he moight git the bounce ef he took aff his hat to anybody whoile he wuz settin' an the box. He said ther Misses didn't allow her coachman to bow to them wat they know —noice manners thot they teach among the 'upper ten,' phwhat?"

"Och, Mrs. Mulhooney, the loike wuz never heerd tell av before——An phwhat's ailin' the goat? Niver a-wunst did he offer to run at me whin Oi kim in!"

"Willie's bin ailin' since this toime lashst Chuesday, whin he ate moy hat. The hat pins 'll show t'rough his skin soon, an' thin Oi'll pull 'em out wid a monkey-wrench."

"Mrs. Mulhooney!

"But shpakin' av pullin' remoinds me av me brudder's cousin. She's just baught the foinest sit av teeth iver owned in our family. Siveral av her teeth wuz givin' her pains, an' she conceaved the plan to hov 'em all pulled, which she done. Her new ones wuz four months a makin', an' their cost yez will doubtless observe in nixt wake's 'Hibernian.'

"But Oi must be aff, Mrs. Mulhooney. Oi shuppose yer goin' to do honor this avenin' ter the return av Mr. O'Blather, by lindin' yer prisence ter the occasion av his lecture."

"Boy rights Oi am, Mrs. O'Conner, fer Oi hare thot O'Blather's not on'y the coming man, but thot he's came. He's bristed the ocean wave in search av knowledge, ain't he?"

"He hov, an' we'll all turn out ter welcome him back ter the land av Oirish stews an' politics."

"Well, since yez must be lavin' Oi shuppose ye'll depart, Mrs. O'Conner. It's damp weather, an' Oi hope the rain do not effect yer spirits."

"Oi nivir mix dhrinks, Mrs. Mulhooney, t'anks. Oi kape the cork in me spirits bottle this weather, so the water do not dhrip in t'rough the neck. Good day."

O'Blather's Lecture on "Arnitholology"

O'BLATHER. THE ORNITHOLOGIST.

"ARNITHOLOLOGY is wan av the best known methods av shtudyin' burrids an' their customs," said Mr. O'Blather, addressing the cultured meeting assembled to hear his learned discourse on *feathered fowl.*

Shamrock Alley elite were in attendance that evening to do honor to Mr. O'Blather's return from "furren paarts." He had been on a business trip to India,* he explained by way of introduction to his discourse, and, "Whoile in the heathen land," (a stay of some four days,) he had undertaken "the shtudy av the burrid which in India flourishes in profusion."

In an appropriate and poetical manner, Mr. O'Blather first touched upon the "Burrids av beauty an' av sang." In this connection he said:

"The burrids av sang are plentiful in their rarity. They flourish manifold an' numerous.

---

* The nature of Mr. O'Blather's business trip may be explained in that he had shipped for the round voyage, in the capacity of stevedore, on an eastern bound tramp steamer which touched at Ceylon.

"Firrist there is the mocking-burrid thot can ape any other burrid's voice an' intonation better thon any ape can ape a monkey, which, ez yez all know, is great at impersonations an' imitations. In truth, the mocking-burrid is to the race av feathered fowl what the hyena is to the race av quadruped four-footed bastes. As moy learned listeners doubtless know, Oi will not tell them thot 'hyena' manes in Indian to imitate, or above imitation—'hy' maneing above, an' 'ena' maneing any—above any, *or* above any at imitation; fer ye know thot to thranslate a thrue maneing, yez must always lave some word to the imagination, an' then put it in to make sense—"

A unanimous murmur of admiration arose from the spell-bound audience at this philosophical and apparently logical explanation; and thus encouraged, Mr. O'Blather continued:

"Far be it from me, ladies an' gentlemen, to extemporize an the hyena's lonely laugh, or av how he imitates the crying av an innocent babe in the torrid desert. The hyena is a king av imitators; he is an actor among bastes, but the mocking-burrid is his superior, an' it's av *burrids* Oi am shpakin'. Faith, the mocking-burrid is a burrid, an' then there is a cock-or-two (cockatoo) an' a screech-owl.

"But the purtiest songster av thim all is the chicken-patty. There is always a rayson fer the namin' av a species, an' Oi nade not tell yez afther whom the chicken-patty is called; fer av course, yez hev all heard tell av the world-wide lady singer, Mrs. Patti.

"Now, the chicken-patties are the religious burrids av the natives, who, though heathens, are great worshippers in their own pagan fashion. The chicken-patties are kept in the temples, where they are the swate imblems av musical harmony, peace an' love."

On being interrupted and asked by one of his interested hearers to "give a description of a chicken-patty," Mr. O'Blather appeared for an instant disconcerted. But he quickly regained his self-command, and, drawing himself up to his full height, announced with dignity and grave enthusiasm that "the chicken-patty wuz beyond description."

Then, apparently annoyed at the untimely interruption, Mr. O'Blather paused. On being urged by his hearers, he condescended to proceed, however.

"The chicken-patty is the swate imblem to the Indian temple as the dove is the howly imblem av the Christian church.

"An', whoile touchin' an temples, it would be appropriate to till yez av the burrids av prayer. In English these very burrids are called carrion, an' they do carry on outrageous at the temples, though the prastes niver shtop thim, fer they call thim howly. There niver is a wake in this pagan land, fer all the dead corpses are placed soide by soide an the walls av the temples, where they becomes pray fer the burrids av prayer what picks them to pieces wid heart-rendering shrieks."

Here another of the audience interrupted, and asked the lecturer if he did not mean birds of prey instead of birds of prayer: he stated that he kept a bird store, and merely inquired for information.

Still another of the interested hearers piped up and said, "Hy'r lave aff about burrids, an' tell us av the Indian war-dance."

A more inopportune interruption could not have occurred. Mr. O'Blather grew furiously indignant, and stated that he would close his lecture "Widout further comment." And which he did, first stating that "Indian war-dances do not occur in the Oriental East, but only take place among the *untamed* Indians av America's woild peraries."

But while three of the audience had been so ill-bred as to interrupt the lecturer, the others had lis-

tened with profound attention. However, none now
urged Mr. O'Blather to exercise further his powers
of oratory. So Mr. O'Blather descended from the
platform. And he was soon one of the merriest par-
takers of the feast of beer and cheese that followed,
at his expense.

Later, when daylight trickled in through the smoky
windows of the saloon, it found many of O'Blather's
guests still making merry. Upon one of the ladies
sweetly asking the Indian Ornithologist to again tune
up his lyre, he refused by murmuring that he felt
"too full for utterance."

He, however, finally did condescend to sing a short
ballad, which he stated to be the most sacreligious
and soul-offending of all ballads to the turbaned Indian. It was against the sacred bird of India, the
chicken-patty, he announced in awe-inspiring voice;
and then he slowly chanted,

> "Oh the chickens grow so tall
> Thot they kill them in the fall,
> And they eat them feathers and all,
> Down in Bombay."

At the conclusion three cheers were given for
O'Blather, and the party broke up.

A Petition from Dwellers in Shantytown
to have Mention made of them
in the Newspaper

"WITNESS OUR SIGNACHEWRS."

TO the Reporters:—"Iverybody takes their hat aff to me" has nothin' to do wid the question in this case.

Why in the divil do yerz high-flown reporters always publish all "society news" among the big bugs, an' niver so much as mention wan av our names?

Shure'n this is a free country, ain't it, an' hoven't we as much av a roight ter be in the paper as the next feller?

We hov', indade!

Faith, an' didn't we rade in last Monday's paper a long article about a Miss Wayup givin' a house party out to the Divil's Inn* (is it they call it?), and didn't the article tell the names av ivery wan prisent?

Yis, indade; ayven to a Mr. and Mrs. Cook, which is the stylish way, we suppose, thot yez make mention av the cook and his woife!

Now, an the other hand, there's Pat O'Conner, who is just afther givin' a Wake, in commemoration av his dead Grandmother (the Lord rest her soul), the loikes av which has not been surpassed in grandeur,

* Devon Inn.

for years, in this paart av the town. Not wan word did yerz publish about thot in yer blamed society news.

We also obsarve, wid great sarcasm, thot we read wid pleasure the names av all the stayers down to the seashore last week, an' the McMurphys an' McGuires who wor resoidin' at the Wayside Inn, wor niver mentioned at all.

These are only some illustrations av a big problem which is worryin' us *Americans* down here greatly, an' unless we see our names in the "society news" pretty soon, the whole entoire population av' Shanty-town will niver so much ez look at yer blamed paper again.

If, likewise, also, at ony toime, wan av you reporters should want to become a policeman, we'll make it hot fer him.

Witness our signachewrs:

> JAMES McGINNIS,
> BILLY McGUIRE,
> TOM O'CONNER,
> (The brother of Pat who gave the wake.)
> PATRICK MURPHY,
> TIM SEELEY,
> McFEE O'REILEY.

MIT VRIENDS

Remember Und Take Varning

"VON DAY VILE TEMPORIZING ON A MORALIZING BLAN."

VON day vile temporizing
On a moralizing blan,
It shtruck me, how der shky grows dark
Chust pefore der rain pegan.

Dere's someding alvays varns vone,
Like an afterwards pefore:
Like der motion ohf a moving
Heralds slamming ohf a door.

A rattle-snake does rattle
As it goils to take a spring;   .
Und a bee does do some buzzing
Chust pefore it tries to sting.

Remember und take varning
Vrom dese blain und simple vördts,
Dot a someding alvays happens
Pefore Happening occurs.

33

Advice to a Newspaper Reporter from
"Von Grand Vriend ohf Der Profession"

ADVICE TO A NEWSPAPER REPORTER FROM "EIN FRIEND."

EIN reporter's life vas von grand series ohf oxciting coincidences und adventures in Bohemia—don't em? Ain't it? Is it nod?

Der reporting race vas ein schmall vite race py demselves, coming originally from dot land Bohemia, but now mostly Creoles.

Der brincibal raquirement of ein reporter should pe to have von strong institutions und blenty of realistic seashore sand; der rest vas gained py hard oxperiences und dimes, outside ohf, on top ohf, underneath —don't 'em?

Der reporter's politics vas not his own, as dey vas governed entirely py dot party which is nod in der box; or, in odder vordts, he must vote for nobody somedimes und somebody no dimes!

Games vas good recriations, aber der fellows vat plays ball mit dere feet make me feel like I vas on poard ship in onbleasant vedder! Dis vorldt vas full of laziness und shtupidity, aber der latter does somedimes go der former pefore! It don't vas efery plack,

37

threatening cloud your head ofer vat makes you put up your umbrella; likewise, also, vat?

I vill here state, howsomefer, dot I pegan mit der intentions of ending somedime, und der dime has came! Dese vas hardt dimes—don't 'em? Der vonce vas plenty—ain't it? Haf lots ohf cheek und act as if you vas living in Gaul!

Concluding vas not easy ven interesting, aber I must stop! "Der column vas chust completed." So good-pye until·yesterday.

An Heiress

"VE SUFFERED MIT SHIP DISEASE."

IN sommer ven die sun game up
It vos apout vour o'clock.
Mein frau und me, ve used to rise
Mit der growing ohf der cock.

But now I've got lots ohf money
Und a fine, spanking daughter.
I t'ink I glose mein shop, und take
Mein child agross de vater.

So up ve packs und 'vay ve goes
A sailing over de seas.
Upon de ocean vide, rolling,
Ve suffered mit ship disease.

Landed. Ve done der goudinent,
Meinself und mein frau und girl.
Und den ve vent to Gross Britain
To find a duke or an earl.

I reads an advertisement: a
Lady in society
Vould, vor a stated sum baid down,
Gif girls nodoriety.

I answered de advertisement,
Und de lady sent vor me.
I handed her von hundred pounds.
Den she gave mein girl a tea.

But such a growd ohf dudes und gawkes
I nefer pefore haf seen
As game in to meet de heiress.
I t'ink dey t'ought I vas green.

Mein daughter, she got disgusted
Mit de parties, fêtes und teas,
Dough she got lots ohf proposals
Vrom nobles, upon deir knees.

She didn't care vor Englishmen,
Deutsch or Union men vas pest.
Ve grossed pack to America.
Shall I tell to you de rest?

Vell, mein daughter's not yet married.
She's refused a Count vrom France.
I really don't know vat to do!
Von't *you* gome und take a chance?

MEETINGS OF
THE GRAND WATERMELON-PATCH
DEBATING SOCIETY

An Interrupted Debate on the Woman's Rights Question

AN INTERRUPTED DEBATE.

TO dose gaddered in Conbersation Hall dis ebenin', I hab pleasure in introducin' de 'baters ob de occasion," quoth the master of the ceremonies, a tall, solemn looking negro.

His announcement was greeted by a flutter of excitement among the audience: gossipy grannies and ogling damsels craned their heads forward to catch the first glimpse of Mr. Speak Easy, the brilliant but opposing candidate for the honors of the evening. Mr. Speak Easy stepped out upon the platform, and made his bow of acknowledgment to a welcome of very faint applause. He appeared as representative from the Philadelphia Anti-Blumer Club, an organization in small favor down Colored Street. But he *was* a city swell.

Mr. Philander Wampus Winslow, the popular member of the Watermelon-Patch Society, was next presented. He was a fat, jolly man with a countenance as black as anthracite. The visitor was accorded the courtesy of the floor for the first twenty minutes; but he declined, stating that he preferred to hear the argument of his opponent before making any remarks himself.

Brother Philander therefore arose, and a stamping of feet and clapping of hands caused him to refrain from speaking for some moments. As the noise subsided he cleared his throat with excessive violence, and, striking a dramatic attitude, began:

"De woman's rights women.
 Dey has but one song:
 Dey wants all deir rights, an'
 Dey wants to right wrong."

Mr. Speak Easy sprang to his feet. "Pardon me, Mistah Chairman," he interrupted, "ef I venture to conjecture that the ladies' rights subject does not touch upon the question of penmanship. Did I not understahn' mah worthy rival to say that the ladies possessed the desire to write wrong?"

"Not at all, sah," exclaimed Brother Philander, indignantly.

The chairman stumbled to his feet and asked,—

"Jest what did you say, Philander? I am regretfulling, but I disremembah."

Philander chuckled: "Guess you wuz 'bout dozin' off; I'll repeat et fo' youah obligation."

A gaudily dressed negro rose in the audience. "Dey wants to right wrong ob co'se," he said. "We all undahstan's! An' dat's all ets needed."

A fat, old woman, a few seats removed, nodded her wooly head approvingly. "Da's a mighty brainy poem! Mighty brainy! Mistah Winslow's gwyne ter *win* dis hyar 'scussion suah!"

Brother Philander repeated the four lines of his verse slowly and with much emphasis; and, as he concluded, the women of the audience screamed in their enthusiasm and delight.

Mr. Chairman stepped to the front of the platform; his manner was very nervous as he turned partially around so that the sweep of his vision might include Mr. Speak Easy as well as the audience.

"Ah trust," he said, "dat dere'll be no disturbance. Fo' none ain't necessitous. Mistah Speak Easy is hyah dis ebenin' at ouah invitation. We challenged his club to a 'scussion upon de great question ob de day, an' his club sent him to represent dem in de ahgument. Now, ef et ain't agreeable to ouah folks to heah Mistah Speak Easy's 'bating, et ain't necessitous fo' us to listen. But on de same reason dere ain't no occasion fo' violence."

A great, burly negro, at a far end of the hall, sang out,—

> "Come aroun' some oder night,
> Fo' dey's gwyne ter be a fight,
> Dere'll be razors a flyin' in de air."

Mr. Chairman raised his hand, and called, "Silence!" Then he addressed the representative of the Anti-Blumer Club.

"Mistah Speak Easy, yo' know de motto ob ouah society is 'Woman's Rights.' So you's rubbin' us on a sore place when yo' runs up against ouah motto. We's a high-spirited lot ob niggahs down 'n dis localitation, an' Ah reckon dat we can't keep calm in hearin' ahgument agin ouah motto. Ef yo' will do us de kindness to subsist f'om youah recitation, howevah, we will call de 'bating off fo' dis ebenin'."

Mr. Speak Easy agreed to the proposition; he had the good sense to see that numbers were against him.

Brother Philander Wampus Winslow's
Discourse on "De Modern People
Am Exactly Laike de Ancients"

BROTHER WAMPUS WINSLOW'S DISCOURSE.

ON the night of the next meeting of the Grand Watermelon-Patch Debating Society, Conversation Hall was filled to overflowing.

Deacon Jeremiah Jefferson delivered a long address, the subject of which was "De Modern People Am Not Laike de Ancients." He resumed his seat with the air of the self-satisfied victor to whom "honors are easy." And he awaited the contradictory delivery of his opponent, Brother Philander Wampus Winslow.

The latter arose with considerable deliberation, and, eyeing the audience with a very knowing expression, said,—

"Leddies an' Gemmen: I'll begin mah ahgument by sayin' dat what Deacon Jeremiah Jefferson said ain't true, owin' ter de fact dat Samson war laike unto a great modern actor, 'kase he brought down de house; dis sayin' am entirely original, an' am chose fo' de

53

express purpose ob illustratin' de fact dat 'de modern people am exactly laike de ancients.'

"De odder day I heard a feller say dat he t'ought cinnamon war de great spice; but, leddies an' gemmen, I considah nutmeg greater (grater).

"Somebody sez dat a niggah's skin ain't exactly black, but de feller what sez dat am color-blind in my opinion.

"A great question once riz as to weddah de mos' finest gals got married or stayed single; an' it war decided dat de mos' finest gals stayed single. Now I beg to differ, an' say dat mah observation has been dat de mos' finest gals get married; but I'd laike to add dat I don't tink de gals' fadders realize deir value when dey 'give dem away.'

"Mah grandmodder used to be a bery good woman when she was on dis firmament; an' one ting she was bery interested in waz sewin'. She sewed lots fo' de poor, until one day a tramp come along, an' goin' up to mah grandmodder, he took a button out of his pocket, an' said: 'Please sew a shirt on dis fo' me.' She nebber done no moah sewin' fo' de poor after dat; so I gib you dis motto: 'Doan hab cheek.' An' now, leddies an' gemmen, mah sayin' am said; but go away wid mah discourse printed upon de paper ob youah hearts, an' nebber let nobody say agin dat de modern people ain't laike de ancients."

Brother Philander Wampus Winslow resumed his seat amid a clamor of applause, and when Deacon Jeremiah Jefferson arose to renew his argument, he was hissed and jeered while the people cried,—

"Samson am laike de modern actor 'kase he brought down de house."

At this juncture the Judge arose, and, calling silence, announced that Mr. Philander Wampus Winslow had made "de mos' finest speech," and had, therefore, won the debate. He concluded by saying: "I will add dat I am requested to gib de following notice: 'De Guild fo' de Prevention ob Cruelty to Chickens will meet here next Wednesday aftahnoon, at foah o'clock, an' Miss Raspberry Rosetree will be pleased to see membahs ob de flock at her house on next Tuesday aftahnoon, to meet seberal membahs ob de Gran' Watermelon-Patch Society.' "

At the Theatre—
From the Gallery Standpoint
and
Politics

WITH GRACE WELL BEFITTING THE WINNERS IN THE CAKE WALK.

MR. OBADIAH SHINBONE LINCOLN was attired in his best Sunday clothes as he led his beaming spouse to a seat in the "peanut gallery" with grace well befitting one who had so recently taken first prize in the "Grand Philadelphia Cake Walk." When the asbestos curtain began slowly to ascend, a small boy sitting next to Mr. Lincoln leaned eagerly forward, but was quickly pulled back again by a man who demanded, in a stern voice,

"Now, mein leedle Jakey, vat vor you get so oxcited ven de fire-proof gurtain goes up, ain't it?"

"O fader," the boy replied, "I alvays like to get me der most for mein money, und I vant to see all vat dere is to be seen, vrom de peginning to der end!"

This answer seemed to please the father, who patted his son on the back and murmured,

"Leetle Jakey vill make ein great peeseness man some day!"

"Good avening, Mister Morgenstein, faith an it's yourself is it, thot I see at the theaythre?" said a jovial-looking Irishman, who was just about to take the seat next to Mr. Morgenstein.

59

"Ah, Meester Fitzgerald, it don't vas glad I am to see you, und how fine und nobby you do look in dem pants; vy dey fits you like der paper on der vall, und I also tells you dat you vas strikin' ein grand pargain ven I sold dem to you dis morning!"

"Yes, Mr. Fitzgerald, dem's der pants vat it takes two pairs ohf to show der pattern!" added Jakey enthusiastically.

Further conversation was cut short by the rising of the curtain.

The first act amused all our friends, who sat with wide-open mouths "taking it in;" and when the curtain fell, Jakey Morgenstein and his father clapped and hurrahed, while Mr. and Mrs. Lincoln regarded them with a supercilious smile, and Mr. Fitzgerald roared with laughter until the next act began.

A midnight scene in a graveyard made Mrs. Lincoln shudder and hug close up to her husband, who instantly assumed an unconscious and far-away expression. An Italian, sitting next to Mrs. Lincoln, frightened her all the more by grinding his teeth and muttering to himself whenever the banditti on the stage brandished their long knives.

When the villain stabbed the hero, and the latter fell from a seemingly stupendous height to the floor of the stage, Mr. Fitzgerald exclaimed,—

"O my, but thot must hov hurt!"

And he went off into a fit of laughter which lasted until Mr. Morgenstein touched him on the shoulder and told him in a mysterious whisper that it was not "good peeseness bolicy" to laugh too much. During the following *entre-acte* Mr. and Mrs. Lincoln went out to get some pink lemonade, and Messrs. Morgenstein and Fitzgerald remained in their seats and reviewed the gossip of "Shantytown."

"I haven't seen Tim Flynn av late; phwhat's became av him?" asked Mr. Fitzgerald.

"Ach he vos into mein shop only a veek ago," Mr. Morgenstein said. "He left ein suit ohf glothes und ein vatch mit me, but said he vould gome pack again for dem in a few days. Says he, 'Der height ohf mein ambition vas reached, Isaac; I have begome ein actor since I seen you last.' He said he vas blayin' two barts down to der Standard Theatre."

"Phwhat wor they; 'off an' on?'" suggested Mr. Fitzgerald, with a twinkle in his eye.

"He didn't say oxactly vat der names ohf der parts vas," Mr. Morgenstein continued, taking his friend's question seriously, "but he told me vat he had to do. Says he, 'I vear a heafy suit ohf armor in der first agt; in der segond agt I vear a pirate's suit und gary ein large tin sword in mein hand. In der third act I gome out dressed in der armor again. Der vas ten oder fellers dressed chust like me. Ve have ein captain vat does all der talkin' vor us. In der first agt ve sing ein gorus to a song vat der captain sings der vordts ohf. In der segond agt ve have to make ein lot ohf faces und say, 'Ve vill, ve vill,' ven der captain says, 'Shall ve steal de girl from her fader's home?' In der third agt ve have a 'scrap.' Der captain gets de girl. Ve gif t'ree cheers, und der gurtain valls vile der girl's fader vas doin' ein song und dance.' "

A blank expression was on the face of his listener as Mr. Morgenstein concluded. The speaker himself did not appear to understand the exact drift of what he had just said. The mutual conclusion was, however, that Tim Flynn was on the road to fame and fortune.

When Mr. and Mrs. Lincoln returned to their seats, the former got into quite a spirited discussion with Mr. Morgenstein, who accused Mr. Lincoln of shutting out the view, tramping on his feet, and disturbing his comfort generally, when he and his wife clambered past. During the following act Mr. Lincoln and Mr. Morgenstein continued their discussion in an undertone which, by degrees, grew more lively, and especially so when two little darkies appeared and sang "Ta-ra-ra-boom-de-aye." Mr. Lincoln maintained that it was "a shame fo' respectable colored folks to let themselves be made such fools of by w'ite trash." Mr. Morgenstein wanted to know where the "white trash" was, and he scoffed at the idea that any colored folks were "respectable" in comparison with "der vite gentlemens at der blay."

Mr. Fitzgerald leaned over and made some loud and stinging remarks about "niggers and hen-coops."

At this juncture the actors stopped in the performance, while cries of "Go it there!" "Silence!" and "Put 'em out!" arose from various quarters of the building; Messrs. Morgenstein and Lincoln found themselves the central objects of all eyes.

But Mr. Lincoln felt equal to the occasion. Arising, he leaned over the railing, and thus addressed the audience: "Gemmen and leddies ob dese hyar United States!"

"S—s—sh!" cried the people.

"Oh, I beg de leddies' pahdons, I should hab said de leddies and gemmen; I proceeded wid mah conbersation jess ez ef I war one ob de w'ite folks down dere, fo' I *knowed* dat war de right way to do in de freatre, kase I'se often be'n up'n de top gallery w'en de w'ite folks in de freatre pahties talked so loud dat de people wot war actin' couldn't remember deir own elocutions."

The noise and excitement had become intense. "Put him out! Put him out!" the people cried, and several ushers came rushing towards Mr. Lincoln.

"Guess we'd bettah take ouah departure from dis w'ite trash hole, Saliana!" said the latter to his admiring spouse; and, giving her his arm, the two walked grandly out.

The noise ceased, the audience quieted down again, and Mr. Morgenstein rubbed his hands with delight, remarking to Jakey, "I got der pest ohf der pargain dot dime!"

POLITICS.

"James Mooney, now yew hurry up, an' don't be all day about it neither. My lands, we'll miss thet boat to the picnic, fer sure!——I declare, yew stop to chin with every Tom, Dick and Harry everywhere."

"All right, Minty, but you *would* have me go into politics, an' this is what you get. You told me to make a name for myself. I have to be pleasant to every body so as to become popular against election day . . . "

"How-de-do, Jim. Please gib me ten dollahs. Dere's a pow'ful la'ge fambily down mah way et needs convertin'; dey're dead agin us now, an' a tenner'll bring 'em roun'. Ef we gets 'em, we gets de wahd (ward), fo' dey hab a lot ob fren's dat always relies on dere perlitical jedgment fo' de way dey casts dere votes."

"All right, Sam; don't explain any more. 'Ere's the money. An' 'low me to present you to me wife. Minty, this is Mister Waters."

"I think the boat'll be movin' *over* the waters ef we don't git aboard. I'm goin', an' yew kin foller, ef yew want."

(Mr. Mooney, in an undertone to his wife.) "Say how-d'y, Minty, an' be polite an' cordial, or we'll lose the nigger vote."

"Ah trust mah presence doan gib no offence, Mistah Mooney?"

"Not at all, Sam. Drop round to dinner with us to-morrow." .

Mrs. Mooney grew pale with rage, turned upon her heel, and walked away. Her husband remained a moment to conciliate the negro, explaining that Mrs. Mooney "had one of her spells;" when he rejoined his wife he reproved her for her lack of co-operation.

Mrs. Mooney replied,—"Well, sakes alive, Jim! Did George Washington, er Grove Cleveland, er Julius Caesar, er Patrick Spootendyke ever 'nvite niggers to their family table to git their vote? Ef they did, et ain't in history!"

"There's a good many things wot happened wot ain't *written* in history, Minty."

"Well, may *be*, but I ain't a goin' to hev my family history tarnished by any such acts—"

"It's money I'm afther, an' shure Mooney has it! Ah! Ha! Ha!"

"Why, hello Pat! How much?"

"Tin, ter change the faith av some unbelievers."

Mr. Mooney whispered to his wife,—"It's me last money, an' if I give it to him we can't go to the picnic."

Mrs. Mooney compressed her lips, and then answered,—

"I'll be brave, Jim, an' give up the pleasure. Fer sartain, it's dooty before pleasure; so serve yer country an' pay the price, ef yew think the money's *needed* fer yer cause."

So Mooney's last ten dollars were handed to Pat, the ward-heeler, and Mr. and Mrs. Mooney returned homeward with the prospect of spending a hot Sunday in town, but with the feeling that they had made another speculation in Mooney's rising stock of popularity.

And now little remains to be told. Mooney is at present serving the United States as a full-fledged politician, and he hopes, next term, to be nominated Senator.

His admirers declare that "he is cut out to be the 'Speaker of the House.' " They deem him "a born orator."

To enlarge Mooney's circle of admirers, and to secure for him, if possible, the confidence of the reading public, it might be well to append his famous speech that won for him his first political victory. He wrote and delivered it himself—and here it is:

"FELLOW-CITIZENS:—I do not presume to stand before you this afternoon trusting in my own ability and influence, but trusting rather in the ability and ever-increasing power of our great party." (Applause) "Our party, friends, is like the emblem of our mighty country, the bald-headed eagle.

"As this noble bird first fluttered forth from the grand old State House on the day of the signing of the Declaration of Independance, so our party had its origin. As the power of the great Union increased, and, as its emblem, the eagle, stretched forth its wings and soared into the air above us, so the power of our party grew steadily, both in influence and numbers. As the noble bird received the gory wound, which brought it temporarily to the ground, when the Civil War broke forth, so has our party received set backs during opposing administrations. But these set-backs have only been temporary, my friends. As the noble eagle recovered from its wounds and arose stronger than ever, when the bloody Civil War had ended, so our party has come out victorious and more powerful than ever after its temporary defeats. As the eagle arose triumphant, I repeat, when that great internal eruption was over, and as since that it has risen ever higher, until in the most exalted heavens it finally stretches forth its golden pinions over all the world, so is our party steadily growing. At no distant day I prophesy that it will be the only power in America!

"The great American people is composed of two classes—the laboring men and the business men. Which is the largest and more patriotic class? Who are the true Americans? The laboring men! Our party! The only party!" (Prolonged applause.) "To gain our ends we must have representatives in politics; we must have friends there to look after our interests and to give us a voice in the Government. Now, I do not ask you to vote for me. Far be it from that. But, friends, dear friends, I would die at any moment for the defence of our cause. I know you all, and you are dearer to me than my life. This ward, the greatest ward in our noble city, should be ably represented. Mr. ————, my worthy competitor, who represents the opposing party, is a business man. He lives for his own ends. I am a laboring man. I work for my friends and serve them with heart and soul."

www.ingramcontent.com/pod-product-compliance
Lightning Source LLC
Chambersburg PA
CBHW021514090426
42739CB00007B/602

www.ingramcontent.com/pod-product-compliance
Lightning Source LLC
Chambersburg PA
CBHW021514090426
42739CB00007B/602